This Book Belongs To:
_____

DECEMBER 1

"For to us a child is born, to us a son is given."
Isaiah 9:6-7

Color Your Own Picture Here

DECEMBER 2

"Glory to God in the highest."

Luke 2:14

Color Your Own Picture Here

DECEMBER 3

"Be kind to one another."
Ephesians 4:32

Color Your Own Picture Here

DECEMBER 4

"You are the light of the world."

Matthew 5:14

Color Your Own Picture Here

Color Your Own Picture Here

DECEMBER 6

"Call his name Jesus, he shall be great."

Luke 1:31-32

Color Your Own Picture Here

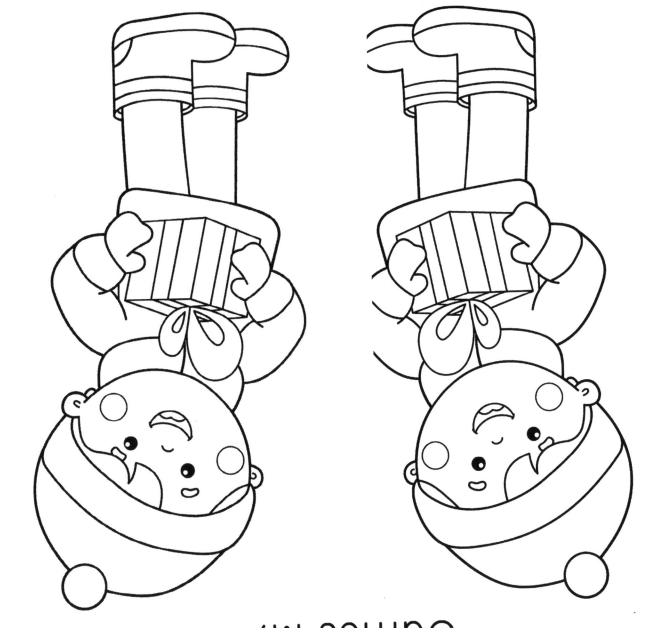

DECEMBER 7

"Every good gift and every perfect gift is from above."
James 1:17

Color Your Own Picture Here

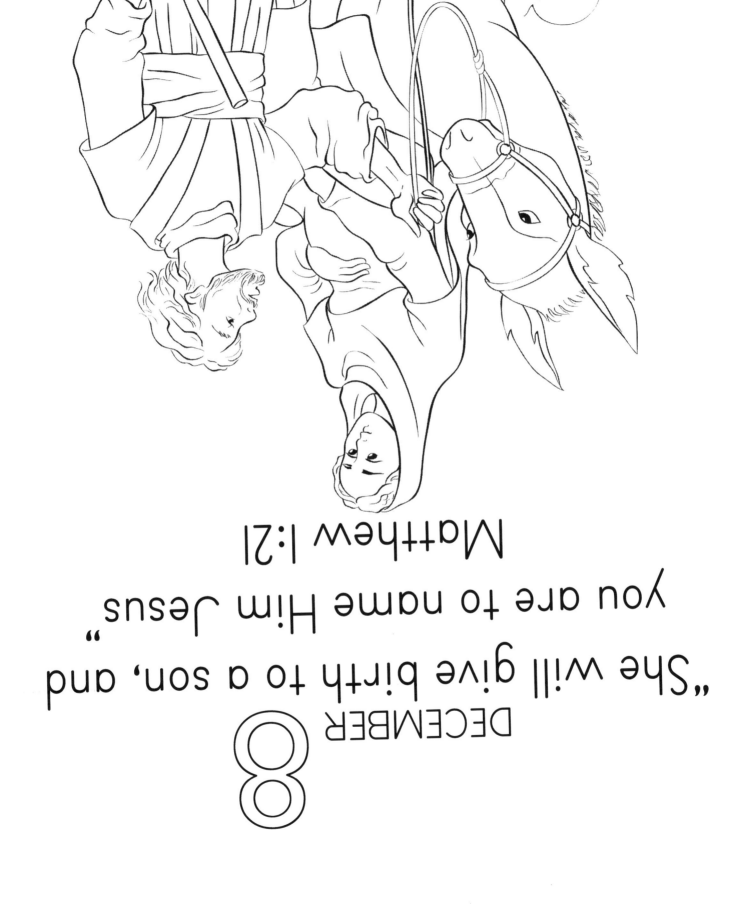

DECEMBER 8

"She will give birth to a son, and you are to name Him Jesus."

Matthew 1:21

Color Your Own Picture Here

DECEMBER 9

"Trust in the Lord with all your heart."
Proverbs 3:5

Color Your Own Picture Here

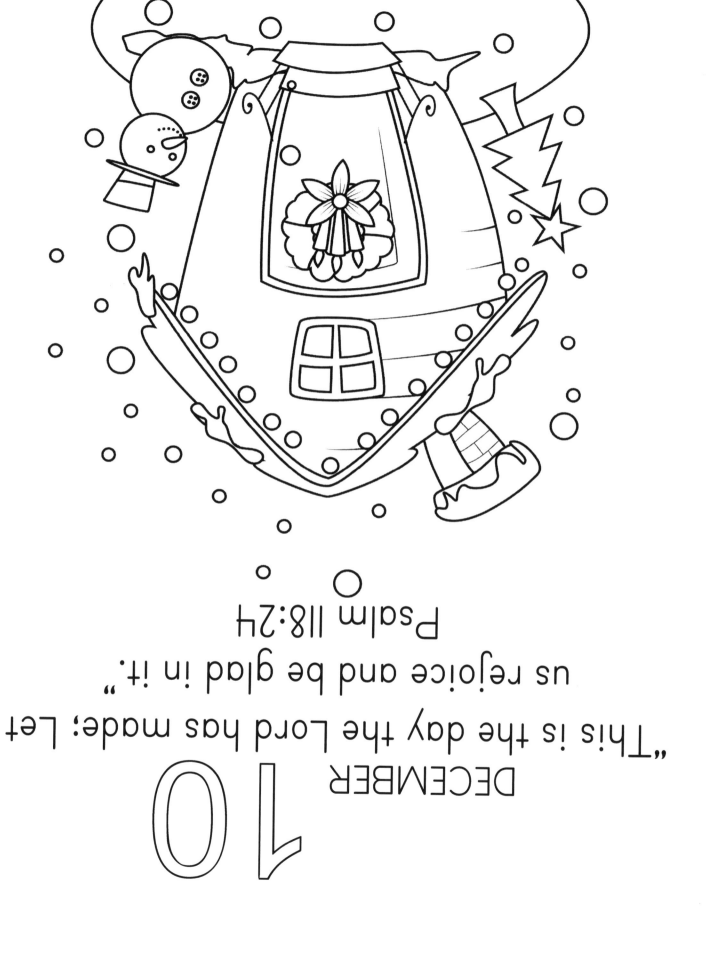

DECEMBER 10

"This is the day the Lord has made; Let us rejoice and be glad in it."
Psalm 118:24

Color Your Own Picture Here

DECEMBER 11

"I praise you God, for I am fearfully and wonderfully made."
Psalm 139:14

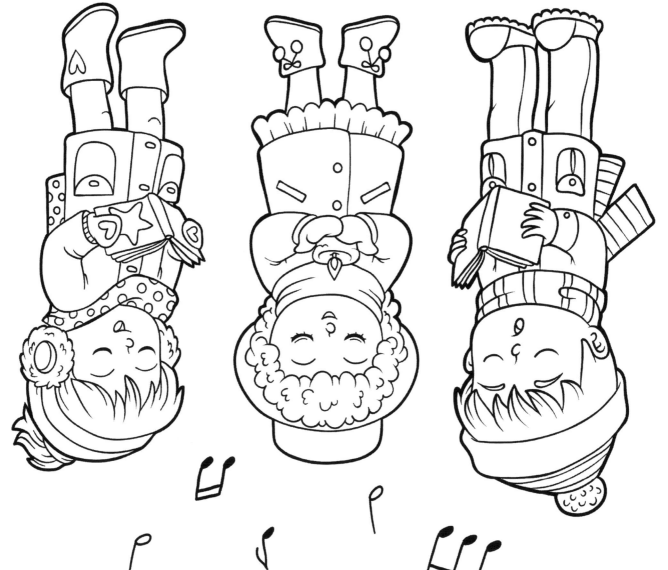
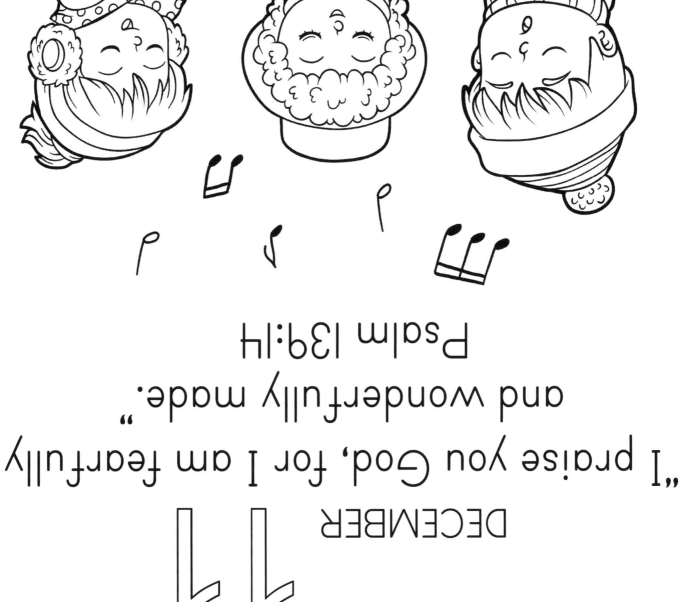

Color Your Own Picture Here

DECEMBER 12

"I am the good shepherd."
John 10:11

Color Your Own Picture Here

DECEMBER 13

"Your word is a lamp to my feet and a light for my path."
Psalm 119:105

Color Your Own Picture Here

DECEMBER 14

"The heavens declare the glory of God."

Psalm 19:1

Color Your Own Picture Here

DECEMBER 15

"Let everything that has breath praise the Lord."
Psalm 150:6

Color Your Own Picture Here

DECEMBER 16

I am with you always.
Matthew 28:20

Color Your Own Picture Here

DECEMBER 17

"I will praise thee with my whole heart."

Psalm 138:1

Color Your Own Picture Here

DECEMBER 18

"In the beginning, God created the heavens and the earth."

Genesis 1:1

Color Your Own Picture Here

DECEMBER 19

"Children, obey your parents in the Lord, for this is right"
Ephesians 6:1

Color Your Own Picture Here

DECEMBER 20

"I am the good shepherd."
John 10:11

Color Your Own Picture Here

DECEMBER 21

"The Lord gives wisdom."
Proverbs 2:6

Color Your Own Picture Here

DECEMBER 22

"Give thanks to the Lord, for he is good; his love endures forever."
Psalm 107:1

Color Your Own Picture Here

DECEMBER 23

"When Jesus spoke again to the people, He said, 'I am the light of the world.'"

John 8:12

Color Your Own Picture Here

DECEMBER 24

"But the angel said to them, "Do not be afraid; for behold, I bring you good news of great joy which will be for all the people"
Luke 2:10-11

Color Your Own Picture Here

DECEMBER 25

"And she gave birth to her firstborn son; and she wrapped Him in cloths, and laid Him in a manger"

Luke 2:4-7

Color Your Own Picture Here

Made in the USA
Monee, IL
17 November 2019